Let

MW01098755

SCHOOL PUBLISHERS

Photos:
p. 2, Map © PhotoDisc; p. 3, Can © fStop/Getty Images; p. 4, © PhotoDisc; p. 5, © ImageClub Graphics; p. 6, © PhotoDisc; p. 7, © Photodisc; p. 8, © Emma Thaler/Getty Images

Printed in China

ISBN 10: 0-15-358367-3
ISBN 13: 978-0-15-358367-4

Ordering Options
ISBN 10: 0-15-358355-X (Grade K Below-Level Collection)
ISBN 13: 978-0-15-358355-1 (Grade K Below-Level Collection)
ISBN 10: 0-15-360620-7 (package of 5)
ISBN 13: 978-0-15-360620-5 (package of 5)

4 5 6 7 8 9 10 0940 15 14 13 12 11 10 09

map

can

fan

Dan

pan

cap

nap